Edgar Cayce and
A Course in Miracles

D1596328

Edgar Cayce and A Course in Miracles

A Comparison of the Teachings of the Edgar Cayce Readings and *A Course in Miracles*

Judith Sherbenou

ARE
PRESS

ASSOCIATION FOR
RESEARCH AND
ENLIGHTENMENT

A.R.E. Press • Virginia Beach • Virginia

A.R.E. Press
215 67th Street
Virginia Beach, VA 23451–2061

Library of Congress Cataloguing–in–Publication Data
Sherbenou, Judith, 1940–
    Edgar Cayce and a course in miracles / by Judith Sherbenou.
        p.   cm.
    ISBN-13: 978-0-87604-568-8 (trade pbk.)
    1. Cayce, Edgar, 1877–1945. 2. Course in miracles. 3. Parapsychology.
4. Spiritual life—New Age movement. 5. New Age movement. I. Title.
    BF1999.S455 2006
    299'.3—dc22

                                2006028948

Cover design by Richard Boyle

Contents

Introduction vii

In the Beginning 1

The Nature of Mind 5

Healing and the Body 15

Love and Fear 23

Judgment and Forgiveness 29

Relationships: Our Arena of Learning 37

Drawing Closer to God Through Prayer and Meditation 43

And in the End 49

Conclusion 53

Endnotes 55

Introduction

$\mathcal{A}$s a student of the Cayce principles since 1969, I have been applying these teachings in my everyday life in a very practical way. I was drawn to the study of *A Course in Miracles* in 1979 and found a fresh source of challenges as I also attempted to put these principles into practice. The two philosophies share a common goal: realization of oneness with God or atonement. In recent years, as I have traveled throughout the Southwest giving presentations on these concepts, people have requested more information that compares the two teachings. This book is a response to that need.

The Cayce material, which is Judaic–Christian in orientation, covers a vast spiritual and philosophical arena. The Course, which is said to be channeled from Jesus in response to two individuals seeking a "better way," is Christian and psychological in form but has a universal message. It focuses on changing the mind as the means of spiritual growth.

This focus is certainly nothing new to the Cayce student, who is often reminded, "Mind is the builder." The understanding that comes from the Cayce readings introduces many Eastern beliefs, such as reincarnation and karma, and makes them work for the westerner. According to Cayce and other sources, Jesus studied in India in his youth, which would, no doubt, have instilled in Him both an understanding and a great respect for the Vedantic teachings. Both Cayce and the Course offer a wedding of Eastern and Western spiritual philosophy at some level.

It is expected that any reader drawn to this book will not be a new-comer to Cayce; therefore, there will be no detailed description of his life and work. For this information, see Thomas Sugrue's *There Is a River* or Jess Stearn's *The Sleeping Prophet*. Similarly, this book is not meant to be an in-depth analysis of *A Course in Miracles*. For a very clear overview see *An Introduction to a Course in Miracles* by Robert Perry or the appendix in Kenneth Wapnick's *Absence from Felicity*. I do not intend to represent my-self as an authority on the philosophy of *A Course in Miracles*, but rather, wish to share my experiences and interpretation with those of similar interests. Indeed, there are already several differing interpretations of the Course material, even among those who *are* authorities.[1]

During his lifetime Edgar Cayce gave more than 14,000 telepathic clairvoyant statements, known as "readings," for more than 6,000 different people. The majority of these were health readings given for people who had, in many cases, given up hope of help from traditional medi-cal sources. In many of these health readings there was as much focus on attitudes as there was on treatment. In addition Cayce gave what are now referred to as "past life readings," which explained the natural laws of cause and effect and provided advice for spiritual development. The philosophy that can be gleaned from these readings is studied and ap-plied in study groups, known as *Search for God* groups, which meet weekly in homes around the world.

While *A Course in Miracles*, scribed by psychologist Helen Schucman from 1965 through 1972, is intended to be an individual study, groups meet for discussion of the material and support throughout the world. Both the philosophy of Cayce and that of the Course are such that un-derstanding and application occurs at deeper and deeper levels as the material is studied.

This book is an attempt to show the Cayce student how the two teachings can support one another and in what areas the two disagree. As the Course itself states, "The form of the Course is not for everyone. There are many forms of the message, which is universal, all with the same outcome. The Course is but one." (M-3) The Cayce material can be seen as another. As Cayce would often say concerning his own words or those of any teaching, try it out. If you find the information helpful when you apply it in your life, incorporate it. Similarly, the Course would advise looking to see if the ideas make you feel more peaceful or less peaceful. Make the choice for yourself.

A *Course in Miracles* undertakes to teach us to let go of all beliefs and concepts that are a part of our world of illusion. The Course itself is admittedly an illusion brought into the illusory world as a "wake-up" call, and will eventually be released along with our belief in all other illusions. A *Course in Miracles* would say this comparison of the two teachings is also an illusion, for true knowledge cannot be compared. Only beliefs, which are temporal, can be compared.

Not all areas of difference in the two teachings will be examined here. For example, the Course views biblical references in a different light than did Cayce. The Cayce material, in teaching how to live a more loving and productive life in service to our fellow man, often utilizes Bible references in substantiation. Cayce regarded scripture as the word of God and used it both in his own life and in his teachings. The Course, on the other hand, conveys that much of scripture was either written by or translated by the ego part of the split mind and is, therefore, unreliable as a guide. Fear-engendering scriptures and those that are divisive were pointed out as not being consistent with Jesus' intentions in teaching about oneness. This Course perspective is, understandably, a threat to those who rely on the Bible as being the word of God. A *Course in Miracles* demands that we give up ALL beliefs and concepts in order to withdraw our investment in the world as we know it.

Numbers referencing the Cayce readings will follow the excerpt, in most instances. The first part indicates the reading number, which identifies the inquirer. The number following the hyphen shows which of a sequence of readings is cited for that person. For example, 294-1 would indicate the first reading for the person identified as "294."

References from the A *Course in Miracles* original three-volume set will be designated as T = Text; W = *Workbook*; and M = *Manual for Teachers*. The example, (T-344) would indicate that the reference came from page 344 of the original A *Course in Miracles* text. This material may also be referred to as "the Course" or "ACIM." Direct quotes from ACIM are limited in number of words by the publishers; therefore paraphrasing the material was a necessity. I do not presume to improve on the Course's beautiful poetic expression.

In the Beginning

*E*dgar Cayce was a devoted Bible student and teacher all his life, and he starts his account of humans' beginnings on earth from the framework of the Book of Genesis: "In The Beginning God created the heavens and the earth." (Genesis 1:1)

According to Cayce, man's first awareness was spiritual, as his first consciousness was in the mind of God. Man was created in the spiritual, rather than the physical image of God.[1] God's desire for companionship produced the "Sons of God," souls who were endowed with free will. The loss of spiritual consciousness was the result of rebellion or selfishness—the partaking of knowledge without wisdom. (817-7) This spirit of selfishness is called by many names—the small self, Lucifer, Satan, and the Devil. *A Course in Miracles* would call it the ego.

The earth began as a spiritual expression of God and was not intended for use by the souls. Cayce described man's entering the earth plane after the creation of the mineral, plant, and animal kingdoms as inspired by curiosity and a fascination with materiality. The souls became more and more curious about the sexual activity of the animals, and they began to experiment by entering the animal bodies. As this experience became more attractive, the souls began to forget their spiritual origins as the children of God. Eventually, the souls found themselves locked into the physical bodies of the animals, unable to come and go as they once had. These souls were trapped into materiality.

The Bible states that "God does not will that any soul shall perish." (2 Peter 3:9) And because God is a compassionate and loving God, a divine plan was devised. The Sons of God who had not fallen and were still in God-consciousness looked upon their trapped counterparts and realized a plan would need to be devised to release the souls caught in their own thought-creations or ego-projections.[2] They surveyed the existing animal forms and selected the one most suitable for the soul's inhabitation and began influencing its evolution to create the form eventually known as "man." (As an interesting side note, this account of the creation offers a wedding of the evolution theory and the creation theory.) This project was headed by the soul later known as Adam and as Jesus.

The Sons of God entered the spiritualized animal form now known as "man" for the purpose of regenerating their fallen consciousness. However, the "Sons of God saw that the daughters of men were fair; so they took them as wives." (Genesis 6:2) This represents the fall of the perfect race. They too were drawn into the temptations of materiality. It was over 200,000 years between the advent of Adam and his return as Jesus.[3]

Edgar Cayce would say that man's experiences in the earth, as well as the solar system, continue to be for the purpose of returning to spiritual consciousness: "The development of the soul to the one purpose, the *one cause*—to be companionate with the *First Cause!*" (903-23) or put more simply: "To know thyself to be thyself, yet one with God." (3003-1)

The Cayce readings state that Jesus, having been through every temptation of material experience throughout his lifetimes (as Adam, Enoch, Melchizedek, Joseph, Joshua, and Jeshua, among others), is our pattern for returning to our spiritual heritage.

> . . . there is nothing in heaven or hell, in body, in mind, or in spirit that He hath not experienced.   954-5

> For the Master, Jesus, even the Christ, is the pattern for every man in the earth . . . For all have the pattern, whether they call

on that name or not; but there is no other name given under heaven whereby men may be saved from themselves. 3528-1

Necessary for this gradual return to spiritual consciousness is opportunity and experience. To give humankind every possibility of regaining its lost heritage, reincarnation or rebirth in varied bodies and circumstance was devised, with the law of cause and effect employed to bring about increased awareness. This requires a sense of time and space, which enables humans to experience the results of their thoughts and deeds in the framework of a sequence. This construct is said to have no reality outside of the material experience.

From the perspective of *A Course in Miracles*, God did not create the world we see, the universe, or anything else temporal. He created only that which is true and real, and truth and reality are changeless. God extended Himself, in the creation, as His Son, giving to Him the same will to create, and creating Him perfectly. The Course considers all of God's creation as the "Son of God." The Sonship was given the power to create but only as God would create or extend. God's son can and has used his own creative power inappropriately by projecting. This occurs when man mistakenly believes in some lack and that he can fill this lack with his own ideas instead of truth. These projections are of the ego and are, therefore, illusions. The Garden of Eden represents the pre-separation condition and was a state of mind in which nothing was needed. (T-14) ACIM reminds us that "the Bible says that a deep sleep fell upon Adam, and nowhere is there reference to his waking up." (T-15) As he slept, "A dream of judgment came into the mind that God created perfect as Himself. And the dream was Heaven changed to hell, and God made [an] enemy unto His Son." (T-577)

A Course in Miracles, therefore, sees the so-called fall of man as the mistaken belief that man is capable of separating himself from God. Since this mistaken thinking can only be corrected in the present, ACIM de-emphasizes the past or future and, therefore, does not utilize an understanding of reincarnation as a necessary tool for the return to the awareness of the oneness:

In the ultimate sense, reincarnation is impossible. There is no

> **past or future . . . Reincarnation would not, under any circum-**
> **stances, be the problem to be dealt with now . . . [however] If**
> **(man) . . . is laying the groundwork for a future life, he can still**
> **work out his salvation only now . . . There is always some good**
> **in any thought which strengthens the idea that life and the**
> **body are not the same. (M-57)**

The eating of the fruit of the tree of knowledge is a symbol for man's belief that he can usurp the ability for self-creating. (T-45) The wrong-mindedness that allows man to believe he is separated from God also generates an extensive belief system, which is wholly illusionary. The Course, therefore, is designed to debunk the world of illusion created by the ego and return man to the state of right-mindedness, making possible the oneness with God. The world, according to ACIM, is an illusion created by our separated thinking. We are unable to see it or anything else as it really is because everything we see is tainted by an erroneous belief system that relies on perception rather than truth. "It is impossible not to believe what you see, but it is equally impossible to see what you do not believe." (T-192) Perception did not exist before the separation. (T-37) Perception is outside the realm of knowledge that comes from within. (T-36)

The ego is the symbol of separation, and the Holy Spirit is the symbol for peace. The Holy Spirit has the task of undoing the ego's work. (T-73) Reinterpreting what the ego made, the Holy Spirit sees the world as a teaching device. (T-74) Since we cannot cancel our past perceptions and errors alone, God offers the atonement (T-75), and much of the Course is aimed at preparing the student for this step.

The teachings of the Edgar Cayce readings and those of ACIM do not agree on the origins of the material world. They do, however, agree on the ultimate outcome of man's experience—that of changing the conscious-ness to affect the awareness of the oneness (atonement) with God. In the following chapters we will see how this transformation is to be accom-plished, both through life experience and through spiritual assistance.

The Nature of Mind

*T*hroughout the Cayce readings we often find the statement: "The spirit is the life, the mind is the builder, the physical is the result." This would seem to indicate that the spirit is life itself, and therefore, enlivens all. The mind utilizes this life energy according to the individual's consciousness and produces the physical manifestation in materiality. This means the mind is the aspect of our nature that enables us to be a co-creator with God[1] It is the "spark of the Maker." (3744-1)

The mind itself, though one, can be better understood if seen in terms of functions or levels. Cayce talked of the conscious, the subconscious, and the superconscious aspects of mind.

The conscious mind is described as "that that is able to be manifested in the physical plane through . . . the senses." (3744-1) That is to say our senses make it possible to be conscious. In Cayce's construct the conscious mind is associated with the personality.

He further described the subconscious as the mind of the soul. It operates as a storehouse and can be associated with habit. The subconscious mind does not have the faculty of discernment, and therefore, does not challenge information fed by the conscious mind. The modern analogy of comparing the subconscious to a computer is appropriate here as is the adage "garbage in; garbage out." This is an important element in understanding the use of the mind as the builder. What we dwell upon becomes the material for manifestation. What we believe in, we tend to manifest. The Course would tend to corroborate this concept, and more will be said about this later.

Cayce continued with an additional concept of the function of the subconscious by saying that when the conscious mind sleeps, the subconscious becomes the conscious mind of the soul, and the superconscious then becomes the subconscious. This, then, allows guidance and direction from the superconscious level to reach the subconscious level, sometimes producing dreams containing wisdom from Spirit. This is possibly also an avenue of direct guidance, which can come through during meditation when the meditator is successful in setting aside the conscious mind for a period of time.

Cayce describes the superconscious mind as:

> . . . the divide, that oneness lying between the soul and the spirit force . . . [it is] not of earth forces at all [and is] only awakened with the spiritual indwelling and acquired individually.   900-21

> The superconscious mind is of the Spirit and is one, that is, at one with the mind that is all. It is at this level that we can experience the oneness with God or Creative Forces. This is the mind level we endeavor to reach in meditation. Cayce seemed to be saying that this level of mind is gradually awakened through the setting of an ideal of the highest and through conscious choice to align with that ideal in mental and material experiences.   3492-1

Minds are also joined at the subconscious level, which is what allows thought transfer when the conscious mind is set aside. (900-23) The subconscious is aware of this connection and can be said to "perceive" that all minds are joined. The following is a true experience that illustrates this:

A woman who was learning to meditate had not been warned to start the practice in short time periods. She was well into the second hour of her first meditation when a dialogue began between her conscious mind and the subconscious. The latter proclaimed, "You said I was a failure."

She thought in response, "No, I said that about my cousin."

The subconscious voice continued, "You said I was too fat."

The woman considered that, and then responded, "No, I was talking about my aunt."

This inner dialogue continued for a few minutes until the woman realized that the subconscious mind records as truth about the individual all that is said or thought about self or others because it knows no others! The personal message for the woman was that her continuous criticism of others was hurting her own self-esteem as her subconscious was adding the judgments to the data bank of evidence against her own worth. This brings us to the topic of consciousness building.

Consciousness

According to the Course "consciousness" is a relative term, and therefore, part of the illusion. However, one area concerning the use of the mind in which there is agreement between Edgar Cayce and *A Course in Miracles* is the way in which consciousness is built. "Teach what you want to learn" is a theme commonly repeated in the Course. The meaning of this statement is that we must demonstrate whatever we want to build into our consciousness. Cayce said, " . . . for only that ye have given do ye possess!" (1318-1) He further stated that " . . . unless the experience is thine own to thine own soul, it is only theory." (473-1)

The choice of what to teach is again a matter of the ideal or purpose selected for the life experience. Cayce said:

> . . . all of the good, all of God, all of bad, all of evil that ye may know, is within thine own self. Thus it depends upon what spirit, what purpose, what hope ye entertain as to whether that

> **ye desire to accomplish in thy experience is to be accom-
> plished or not...**   **5164-1**

Choice is emphasized in ACIM as we are admonished: "Teach only love, for that is what you are." (T–87)

Recognizing the oneness, the Course points out not only the method of raising our own consciousness, but also that of raising our brother's along with ours. In practice this means recognizing your brother as yourself and seeing the Spirit as the only reality in yourself. Cayce advocated this practice as well, instructing us to see the Christ in our brother, no matter what the outward appearance may be:

> **For while flesh and blood that is of the earth may not know
> glory, the real body [the spiritual] may become aware of its
> presence in the Presence of the body of God and among its
> brethren... a portion of the whole.**   **987-2**

The goal of raising the consciousness then, according to both Cayce and ACIM is to see the spirit rather than the flesh. "You see the flesh or recognize the spirit. There is no compromise between the two." (T–614)

The Course has an oft-repeated line: "All that I give is given to myself." This statement, again, is emphasizing that what we give IS given to ourselves. Evidence of this is not so easily visible in the material world but at the level of the mind. Cayce said, "Only that which ye give away, only that which ye *live thine own self, is thine!*" (315-5) Cayce continues, "Show mercy that ye may have mercy shown. Show patience that ye may indeed become aware of thy relationship to Him . . . " (1472-12). And, words of truth (life, love, God) make for spiritual growth just as food makes for physical growth and "is experienced in the consciousness of the soul." (254–68)

According to ACIM, "Either you give each other life or death; either you are each other's savior or his judge, offering him sanctuary or condemnation." (T–440) Remember that " . . . everyone sees only what he thinks he is." (T–437) That is to say we have a choice of improving our own consciousness by seeing the light in others. If we wish to experience more joy, peace, harmony, and love, we do so by living joy, peace, harmony, and love, and by witnessing it in all those we meet day by day. The Course reminds us that no thought leaves the thinker's mind or the thinker unaffected. (T-433)

From both Cayce and ACIM we can conclude that our experience of the world is a result of our state of consciousness, and consciousness is something we choose by thoughts and actions. We can improve the world we see and experience by choosing to think and demonstrate that which represents life rather than death.

A seeker asked the sleeping Cayce what to do to bring more love, harmony, and understanding into the home. The reply was to "LIVE IT, THYSELF." (361-9) The Bible's Golden Rule, "Do unto others as ye would have them do unto you," could be interpreted as saying the same thing. On the spiritual level, we have only what we give away. We teach ourselves higher consciousness by giving it to others. We give it by living it. By living it, we make it our own experience, taking it out of the realm of theory. (473-1) As Cayce said, " . . . for only that ye have given do ye possess!" (1770-2)

The Course says the same thing: "To have, give all to all" and "To have peace, teach peace to have it." (T-98) Love works that way and is a good example to consider. Reflecting on the experience of love, we find that it is most potent, most real when we are giving it rather than receiving it from the outside. If you don't believe that then recall a time when someone loved you and you did not return the sentiment. You may have experienced an uneasiness or guilt, but most likely you could not experience the love sent your way. Whatever we give out we experience *first*, so it is an important consciousness–raising device to give out what we would like to have increased in our awareness.

Cayce taught that we must raise our consciousness through free will or choice of the conscious mind. He recommended doing this through the setting of an ideal. Much attention is given to this process in the study group materials presented in *A Search For God, Book I*, where it is stated that we are "ever striving toward something to worship or something to love."[2] An ideal is something toward which we endeavor and is the motivating force in our decisions and actions. We would want to set our true ideal to the highest spiritual attainment that we can conceive—the oneness with God. Cayce so strongly believed in the value of the ideal that he recommended the ideal be established before we begin meditating. Raising the energies in meditation could prove destructive if we fail to set a high spiritual ideal for their application. The setting of the ideal, then, establishes the level of desired attainment. In turn, it affects every action and thought as we measure our daily life by that yardstick. For example, the woman who set as her ideal "oneness with God" could examine an opportunity to discredit another's religious belief as to whether or not the action would make her feel joined or separated from God. A man with the same ideal might decide against a love affair if he saw that dividing his loyalties did not teach himself about oneness. As we apply our ideal on a daily basis to ordinary life, we increase our awareness and expand our consciousness. The ideal we set determines the spirit in which we live our lives. "And with what spirit we apply, we grow also in mind and body." (3424-1)

The Mind and the Course

A Course in Miracles does not find it necessary to use the familiar description of the mind that breaks it into functions of conscious, subconscious, and superconscious, as popularized by twentieth century psychology. Instead, it describes the mind as the active agent of spirit, supplying its creative energy. The mind is described in the Course as having two parts—one created by God, which is called spirit; the other created by the belief in separation, which is called the ego. Spirit is defined as the part of the mind that is still in contact with God through the Holy Spirit and retains the potential for creativity. The ego, according to ACIM, is an illusion and is only capable of making more illusions.

The Course talked about right-mindedness and wrong-mindedness, stating that the mind can be right or wrong, depending on the choice of voice to which it attunes. When we are in our right mind, we are able to hear the Holy Spirit, God's voice in the world, which teaches us forgiveness and true vision. When we are not in our right mind, we listen to the ego, which chains us to the world, perpetuating our sense of separation from God through divisive perceptions such as sin, guilt, disease, and death. We are taught that we have freedom of choice between the voice of the Holy Spirit and that of the ego, between love and fear. Consciousness is described as being able to receive messages from above or below—either the Holy Spirit or the ego—and it is limited to the perceptual realm. Because the consciousness is transitory and is split, it is of the world of form, unable to reach true knowledge. (M-75, 76)

The ego, which is actually an illusion in itself, since God did not create it, is the maker of all we see in the earth experience. It perpetuates its own existence through an elaborate system of beliefs to which it clings. The ego's only purpose is to perpetuate itself, and it accomplishes this by seeming to offer us whatever we believe we lack. The belief in lack is the cornerstone of the ego's power, for the mind-split, or the "fall of man," occurred when we judged that the unlimited creation of God lacked something. That something that God's universe seemed to lack was "specialness." Rejecting the reality of our oneness, the ego devised the belief in separation from God and from one another. Each of us desired to be the only Son of God; so special that God would reorder the creation to meet our childish demands. Splitting the mind into spirit and ego resulted in a sense of deep guilt, symbolized in the Bible's story of Adam and Eve's realization that they were "naked." The ego's answer to such guilt has been to project it outside, making others wrong in order to avoid feeling the profound aloneness the belief in separation creates. The result has been a world of pain, guilt, fear, and isolation, where humankind continues to apply solutions that do not work to problems that do not exist. The world truly can be said to be the "insane asylum of the universe."

In the face of conflict the ego offers two solutions: one is attack and the other is compromise. When we attack, we are trying to overpower another ego, thinking that if we can do so we are then more powerful and even more special. Choosing the other solution, compromise or bargaining, we agree to give in order to get.[3] This is a common "solution" applied in relationships and business situations and indeed, is no solution at all, because it results in everyone losing.

The ego runs a ceaseless monologue in our minds, continuously judging the world we see in terms of its own projections. If you hear yourself, at this moment, questioning such a voice, know that *is* the one! That is the ego's voice, denying that it is there.

The Holy Spirit, which ACIM calls the "Voice for God," on the other hand, is the "still, small voice." As someone once said, "God is very polite, He never interrupts." Cayce stated, "Know that . . . God . . . works with thee in the earth only upon thy *OWN* invitation." (2437-1) It is necessary to still the voice of the ego in order to hear the Voice for God. The practice of meditation makes this possible as "the memory of God comes to the quiet mind." (T-452) The Course however, goes much deeper than this one solution. It is designed to take us through the process of letting go of old beliefs and seeing things differently, so we learn to continuously choose to hear the voice of the Holy Spirit rather than the prattling of the ego. The Workbook, which offers 365 lessons—a year's worth—is designed to do just this.

The central theme of the Voice for God is one of forgiveness. Forgiveness is the solution to all our problems through the healing of the mind. All that we see and experience in the earth is the ego's projection. We require forgiveness to let go of the projection so that we can see as the Holy Spirit would have us see. Forgiveness allows us to experience love. More will be said on this subject in the chapter on forgiveness. Whenever there is a difference of opinion or a dispute, we are directed by the Course to consult the Holy Spirit. Since we all share the same Holy Spirit, we can all receive the same guidance that joining is more important than the subject of the dispute. This puts all parties in the right mind for resolving the situation with love, thus finding a solution that makes a winner of all concerned.

In comparing Cayce's model of the mind with that of the Course, we could say that the conscious mind and the ego are operating at the same level, though Cayce would describe the conscious mind as teachable whereas ACIM would not say so of the ego. The conscious mind and the ego both are operating at our most limited level of awareness. The subconscious, which Cayce described as a storehouse of patterns and tendencies, could be likened to the beliefs that the Course says determines our projections. The superconscious mind, which Cayce described as our contact with Divine Mind could easily be compared to the part of the mind ACIM calls the Voice for God. In both models, it should be kept in mind that the divisions or functions are made for clarifying purposes and do not, in reality, exist. The mind is one. The descriptions help us to understand how we function in the earth and why we are here.

Healing and the Body

*T*he definition of the physical body is an area in which there is a seemingly broad difference between the philosophy of the Edgar Cayce readings and that taught in *A Course in Miracles*.

The Course, it is to be remembered, is a teaching for the mind. This system regards as real only that which was created by God and which is eternal. The body, which is temporal, is seen as part of the illusory world of form, created by the ego—the split-off part of the mind. The Holy Spirit uses the body only as a learning device for the mind. The body is described in ACIM as the "ego's friend" and not a part of the real being. (T-93) The body's purpose, as seen by the ego, is to perpetuate the illusion of separation, so necessary for the ego's world of fear. Our living in and continuously experiencing the separateness of individual bodies reinforces our belief in the separation from God. Any way in which we draw attention to or use our bodies to make them seem more real, including the manifestation of illness, increases our investment in the temporal or illusory world of the ego. Under the ego's influence, we use our bodies to hide our hatred and guilt and to manipulate others. The idea that the body can be sick is of the ego's thought system, and creates the illusion that the body can control the mind, thus, usurping God. (M-53) Nevertheless, the Course describes illness as a decision

(M–54), and Cayce would agree.

Edgar Cayce, a committed student of the Bible, agreed with the Bible's philosophy that the body is the "temple of the living God" and advised us to "keep it beautiful." (3179-1) The body, which is a companion of the soul only in a particular experience, is to be used in selflessness and to the glory of God. Cayce's readings emphasized the care and nurturing of the body and devoted his life to helping others heal. According to Cayce's readings, "The physical, and the mental and the spiritual are *one*, yet each must be dealt with in and through its own sphere." (4308-1) It is through the physical body that the mental and spiritual bodies express in the material plane. (5481-1) In Cayce's view, the physical body is evidence of inner conditions and consciousness. He advised that we keep the physical body fit so that the greatness of the spirit could more readily manifest. (900–289)

In terms of maintaining good health, a keyword in the Cayce readings is "balance." He advocated a balanced diet of 80 percent alkaline, 20 percent acid-reacting foods, achieved by concentrating on vegetables and fruits and keeping proteins and starches as secondary. He also put emphasis on food combinations. For example, protein and starch together make a combination that is hard for the body to digest. Cayce's readings also suggested balance in activities between work, play and relaxation, and spiritual pursuits.

One of the early *Search for God* study groups of which I was a member was led by a woman who was greatly interested in the knowledge that was to be gained from the study of the physical readings. In that group we experimented with the Cayce diet recommendations, discovering that we felt better and thought more clearly when we ate according to the Cayce recommendations for diet. Our meditations improved and our dreams were more focused when our bodies' energies were not continuously employed with food and chemical assimilation. We discovered that use of one of Cayce's most often used remedies, the castor oil pack, relieved a variety of conditions from stress to indigestion. By personal experimentation we discovered the usefulness of many other natural Cayce remedies. Through application of the information in the physical readings and the study of Cayce's view of the body as a whole, we learned to see ourselves as partners with God in creating health for ourselves.

One of the healing methods mentioned in Cayce's readings is known as the "laying on of hands." I had volunteered to participate as a channel for this method of healing on several occasions, not knowing whether or not I was actually successful. Then I had the opportunity to discover its value for myself. I was removing a tuna and cheese casserole from the oven when the oven shelf gave way, dumping the molten cheese onto my right hand. I immediately plunged my hand into cold water, removing the cheese, but the hand was clearly burned. My inner voice prompted me to do a healing on my hand. I sat down, placing my left hand over the right, went within to my center of knowing, where I go for meditation, and began channeling energy from my left hand to my right hand. I continued this for about five minutes and the pain ceased. I proceeded to clean up the mess and did not give my hand another thought until later, when I discovered one small blister, low on the wrist, outside the area that had received the healing energy. I had succeeded in healing myself from the burn through the laying on of hands!

In defining illness Cayce said:

> . . . when there is the improper coordination between the
> physical, the mental and the spiritual forces, these become
> antagonistic.   4670-1

This imbalance creates bodily illness. Though the spiritual, mental, and physical being is one, Cayce said, " . . . yet may indeed separate and function one without the other—and one at the expense of the other." (307-10) The physical body is an out-picturing of what Cayce called the "physical-mental" and the "spiritual-mental." (2475-1) According to Cayce:

> . . . for, while healing of any nature must be from within, it
> depends upon the attitude taken toward all elements and
> influences within the experience . . . when there is co-ordina-
> tion within self, in the inner self . . . then healing is complete.
>   275-32

This idea about attitudes was observable through a sequence of dreams shared in one *Search for God* study group. A member had several dreams in which her car was in distress. In one dream the doors would not stay closed as she drove her car. In another the car was overheating and steam poured out. The next dream showed her driving a car that was out of control. In another she could not get her car out of the garage. Since the car often symbolizes the physical or emotional body, the group concluded that she was being told that she was leaving herself open for illness and needed to rest. She ignored that advice, saying that her life was just too busy for time out to rest. After that, a series of dreams followed in which she saw her own body in various states of infirmity. She still did not heed the advice until the physical illness became a reality. Then she spent several weeks ill and recuperating. This illustrated to those of us in the group that an illness begins from within, in an attitude perhaps, and can be addressed there. If we do not make the changes on the emotional level, we will eventually face the need on the physical level.

In a personal experience, I discovered that emotional pain not acknowledged can be stored in the body. I was undergoing a Rolfing® series. Rolfing is a form of deep muscle massage, which is done through the use of the elbow, for the most part. My Rolfer was inserting his elbow deeply into my back pain and asking, "What is this pain about?" I would respond with whatever came into my mind. He would then thrust his elbow deeper into the pain and repeat the question. When I finally reached the truth about the emotional source of the pain, it suddenly ceased! This made it clear to me that I cannot hide from the emotional pain I do not wish to face, as it will only surface somewhere in my body as a physical pain. I learned firsthand that physical aches and pains have their source in the mind. As the Course states, "Pain is my own idea." (W-382)

Through his access to past life information in the Akashic records, Cayce was often able to tie a physical condition to a past event or belief. Though most of us today don't have access to the information "recorded on the skeins of time and space," we can go within through meditation to our center of knowing, and access helpful information.

A member of my *Search for God* study group recently underwent heart surgery. A longtime meditator, he took the question of the reason for the need for this experience into meditation. His answer came in the form of a vision in which he saw himself in a past life as a soldier. One of the customs at the time was to remove the heart of slain victims following battle, and he saw himself and others doing this. For him this vision was a valid explanation of his need to experience heart surgery. Apparently, at some level, we see the illness experience as necessary for our own growth and understanding. Possibly, if he had forgiven himself for participating in the ancient heart–removal custom, he would not have had to undergo the pain of heart surgery in the present.

The Course would seem to agree with this possibility, as it teaches that forgiveness is healing. ACIM teaches that anything that is not love is not of God and, therefore, is unreal. Any action or circumstance we perceive that is not loving is the invention of our ego–mind, or the "small self," as Cayce would put it. Through forgiveness we can give up what we perceive, such as illness, and accept God's creation, which is love. Forgiveness is a way of relinquishing the illusions we make. Giving up our illusions is returning to God. According to the Course, healing and atonement are identical. (M–53) Once we accept the atonement we are healed because we no longer see ourselves as outside of God. We cannot experience any discord, including illness, if we are of one mind with God.

I was a volunteer at the Houston Center for Attitudinal Healing, which offered support groups for people facing catastrophic illness. The philosophy of this organization was based on the principles from ACIM. At the Center we accepted the teaching that illness is an illusion, and we practiced seeing one another as well and whole, even though material appearances would say otherwise. As facilitators for various groups, we endeavored to hold the thought of atonement as participants shared the experience of their illness. Rather than giving advice or otherwise reacting to their stories, therefore making their pain seem more real, we maintained an attitude of loving acceptance, creating the space for the experience of joining or feeling the atonement. For example, one evening the group of "Significant Others" began discussing the high cost of medical care. Various members revealed medical debts of hundreds of thousands of dollars. The facilitators' holding the thought of love might have been a contributing factor in the group members opening up to the absurdity of the situation. As the discussion progressed into the sharing of joy, the participants began releasing their worry and fear in laughter. We all left the meeting feeling peaceful and joined, rather than fearful and separated.

Again, the Course teaches that forgiveness and healing are one. Forgiveness involves accepting the reality of God's creation (what IS) and relinquishing the mistaken belief that we can improve on it. The need to forgive derives from our practice of projecting "out there" all that we do not like in ourselves. Forgiveness involves taking back into ourselves all of our projections, which are unreal in the first place, so forgiveness—or healing—is the process of undoing our separation from God. The belief that our body can overpower God IS a belief in the separation. By forgiving and relinquishing our ego's investment in being separate—even to the point of physical illness—we reintegrate ourselves with reality. In reality there is no illness and no need for forgiveness. There is nothing but God and His perfect creation. When I find myself with an illness of any kind, I immediately go to work on forgiving—everything from myself, to the people and conditions in my life.

While ACIM's approach is to change the mind, it does not advocate ignoring or denying bodily needs. It teaches, instead, that all material remedies for illness are a form of magic. That is to say that we are mistaken when we believe that the body makes itself ill, and we are further mistaken when we believe that "non–creative agents" can heal. However, the miracle of healing must be expressed in a form that will not create further fear in the mind of the person receiving the healing. Therefore, using drugs, herbs, or some other means of "healing" is appropriate if that is what the person can accept without fear. (T–20) Edgar Cayce's approach to treatment of disease was similar in that he always individualized recommendations according to the particular needs or understanding of the seeker.

Since the majority of Cayce's psychic readings were given for physical conditions there is a wealth of information regarding remedies and treatments. This information is made available by the Association for Research and Enlightenment, Inc. However, attempts to get the sleeping Cayce to make general treatment outlines, applicable to all similar cases of specific illnesses, were generally unsuccessful. One reason for resistance to this idea was that Cayce always addressed the consciousness of the individual. If the person had a "castor oil consciousness" then castor oil packs became part of the treatment. If the patient had a "surgery consciousness" then that might be a necessary part of the treatment. He was able, in the trance state, to reach out and determine the level of understanding of the individual seeking help and respond in the way most appropriate for that person. In Course terms one could say Cayce was applying the "magic" that would not create fear.

Most of Cayce's remedies and treatments brought gradual healing. This was to balance the amount of time the condition had required to come into form and to bring about progressive healing, assimilated by the individual slowly as the consciousness also changed. Cayce often asked, "What do you want to be healed *for?*" He appealed to the seeker to consider what life changes he or she could make so that the same condition would not be recreated. "When there is coordination within self, in the inner self . . . then healing is complete . . . " (275-32) Cayce's way was to gently bring about a raised consciousness so that the mind need not again create illness in the individual. That might happen through insights gained in viewing a past life situation or in experiencing the results of past thoughts or deeds, brought into form.

A Course in Miracles teaches that the body is neutral and can be used either by the ego or the Holy Spirit, according to our choice. Becoming aware that we have a choice is the first step. When I experience pain, for example, I don't deny the pain, but I do pray for the mind that is creating the pain to be healed. A member of my miracles group puts it, "I have a painful thought." When seen that way, we can recognize that we created the thought and we can re-create it into something peaceful.

The Course describes those "on the path" or "awakening" individuals as "teachers of God." We learn of God by teaching of Him. According to this philosophy, the teachers of God do not make the illness more real by addressing it. Instead, knowing that the Father did not create bodies (form), the teacher of God heals by recognizing that what his brother believes about himself is not true. Since the illness is an illusion created out of the belief in the separation, we heal one another by focusing on knowing that there is no separation from God. This is offering the atonement. Cayce would have described it as "seeing the Christ" in the other person.

Cayce, in his holistic approach, addressed not only the physical condition but also the attitudes, emotions, and experiences that brought the illness into manifestation. Further, he stated:

> **Know that there is within self all healing that may be accomplished for the body. For, all healing must come from the Divine . . . As the attitude, then, of self, how well do ye wish to be? How well are ye willing to cooperate with the divine influences which may work in and through thee . . . ? 4021-1**

The Course teaches that healing is accomplished through the mind. Cayce seemed to be saying the same thing when he referred to the mind coming from the Divine. Therefore, the two philosophies concerning healing are compatible and overlap to some extent. Cayce's method was to work on an illness both from the physical level of form and from the mental level that created the illness. ACIM advocates holding to the truth of wholeness, correcting errors in thought that bring about illness at the level of form. In both schools we see the benefits of changing the mind.

Love and Fear

*A*ccording to *A Course in Miracles* there are only two emotions of which we are capable—love and fear. (T-202) All that God created is in the spirit of love. All else was made by the ego and can be defined as fear. Therefore, all experience other than love is fear, or a call for love or help.

Before the separation, fear did not exist (T-18). The ego's decision that God's creation was not "enough" resulted in an attempted projection outside the mind. In other words, we ejected God from the Garden of Eden, believing that He was withholding something from us. Believing we could actually do that—eject God—has produced tremendous fear and guilt, and is the symptom of our own deep sense of loss. All fear is finally reduced, then, to the basic belief that we have the ability to usurp the power of God. (T-15) The Course further states, "No one who hates but is afraid of love and therefore must be afraid of God." (T-563)

The misperception that there is a power greater than God produces a tremendous amount of guilt. The ego handles this guilt by projecting it outside, onto another person, thing, or institution. After we have placed it outside ourselves we then feel justified in attacking it. We, of course, do not do any of this consciously. It is not hard, however, to find an excuse to attack and a willing participant to interact with us about guilt

23

and fear. So, we attack someone else on whom we have placed our guilt. That person, who has also bought into the same ego game, then returns the attack, also feeling justified. And so, the fear game is sustained. The Course says fear " . . . has many forms, meaningful only to their maker. [Man] peoples his world with figures from his individual past, and it is because of this that private worlds do differ. Yet the figures that he sees were never real, for they are made up only of his reactions to his brothers and do not include their reactions to him." (T-230)

We see and relate to only those who remind us of these images. "Projection makes perception and you cannot see beyond it." (T-231)

How often is it true that the fault we find in another is one that we also harbor? I saw this happening in a recent experience. Another woman and I were disagreeing as to whether or not to change the temperature in the room. She held fast to her experience that the room was too hot, and I insisted it was just right. Suddenly, I saw myself in her and said, "There is room for only one bossy person in this room so I will leave." I do not know if she realized the humor in the situation, but I chalked it up as one more tiny awareness of my own attack game.

The Course suggests that the guilt/attack cycle can be interrupted by our becoming aware and making a different choice. When we realize we are caught up in the game, we can choose once again. We can realize the other person involved is in a state of fear and is calling out for help. If we have difficulty seeing this, we are advised to ask the Holy Spirit to help us see the situation differently. Recognizing the fear in the other person can prompt us to respond with love rather than with anger, which is a common fear-response. When we supply love in the situation the other party can withdraw the fear-response of attack. This, in turn, allows us to do the same. Therefore, the falsely created exchange of attack is nullified.

This scenario is clearly seen in the relationship between the teacher and student. As an elementary art teacher I often find children "attacking" through aggressive behavior directed toward one another or toward me. When I respond in kind and sharply reprimand (attack) the child, the situation is not resolved. It might be suppressed or redirected, but it is not really handled. However, when I respond with love, per-

haps taking the child aside to find out what is *really* going on and deal-
ing with that, then the attack–behavior need not continue. Similarly,
when I make it a point to praise the children (send love), rather than
criticize them (attack), they respond by learning more easily and by
getting in touch with their creativity more readily.

Edgar Cayce's view of attitudes and emotions is similar to what we
have seen in ACIM. In reading 5459–3 he states:

> **Fear is the root of most of the ills of mankind . . . To overcome
> fear is to fill the mental, spiritual being, with that which wholly
> casts out fear; that is . . . the love that is manifest in the world
> through Him who gave Himself the ransom for many. Such
> love . . . faith . . . understanding casts out fear . . .**

In other words, when we replace fear with love, we are allowing God
to manifest in our lives.

When we allow fear to enter our minds, we are forgetting our spiritual origins. Cayce said,

> **. . . for he that is made afraid has lost consciousness of self's
> own heritage with the Son; . . . [when we cast] out fear . . . He
> alone may guide.**   **243-10**

This is similar to ACIM's instructions that we call on the Holy Spirit
to help us see the situation differently.

One of the most often presented concepts in the Course is "All that I
give is given to myself." This relates not only to the concept of one mind
but also to the process of giving. Whatever proceeds from me affects me
FIRST. Similarly, Cayce said, "If [that] built . . . in self mentally has been
anxiety, fear, trembling, hate . . . then indeed there must be turmoil
within thyself." (1632-2) The Course concentrates on the present experience, while Cayce saw life as a continuum with a past that affects the
present and present actions and reactions that affect the future. Cayce
often told an inquirer, "Thus we find again the entity in the present is
meeting itself . . . " One woman was told:

[This entity has fear in the present because her] experiences
. . . through the various appearances have brought those of
fear in many . . . In the present then . . . that which brought fear
in a physical sense will be eradicated through the awakening
in the spiritual application of material, as well as physical
activities.   560-1

The woman apparently had the opportunity in her present situation
to overcome fear in herself through applying newly acquired spiritual
knowledge. It could be said, then, that the fear in which we indulge has
its most long lasting effects in ourselves.

A Course in Miracles talks much about our projection of fear outside
ourselves. Cayce seemed to be describing the same process in a reading
he gave for a woman. He described her as:

One interested in things psychic . . . prone to give power to
influences without self. This causes much of the fear, and [she
gives outside credit to] . . . happenings [rather than] . . . that
[they] have come about from . . . that builded by [her] . . . own
activity. For mind is the builder.   5030-1

The woman apparently experienced phenomenon that she associated with fearful sources, which were, in truth, of her own projection,
whether from the past or the present. She was given the remedy earlier
in the same reading when she is told:

For if [you come] . . . to that consciousness which is a part of
the universal consciousness, that ye abide—in body, mind and
purpose—as one with the Creative Forces, ye are at peace with
the world and have nothing to fear . . .   5030-1

She was being advised to identify with love consciousness rather
than fear consciousness.

Much of Cayce's service in the world was directed toward helping
people with physical problems. In talking about fear in connection with

the physical body, he pointed out that " . . . fear is the greatest drawback in the proper development of any well balanced, normal individual." (554-3) He further stated:

> **Worry and fear being the greatest foes to normal healthy physical body, turning the assimilated forces in the system into poisons that must be eliminated, rather than into life giving vital forces for a physical body.**   **5497-1**

In a more specific case, the sleeping Cayce said, " . . . fear creates anger; anger . . . [hinders] digestion . . . " This has certainly been pointed out by medical science which has discovered that fear puts the adrenals in the "fight or flight" mode, which shuts down the digestive processes. So, if for no other reason, the physical effects should provide motivation for letting go of fear.

The Course declares that love is letting go of fear. Cayce agreed in reading 5735-1, saying, "In casting out [fear], replace rather that of grudge, desire and of hatred . . . with the *love* of the Master . . . " And, in another reading, " . . . forget fears and put the whole trust in the source of life, light and immortality." (4084-1)

Both Edgar Cayce and the teachings of ACIM would seem to agree that fear is the condition in which we find ourselves when we are trusting in the ego, or small self, as Cayce would call it, rather than putting full trust in God. ACIM states that attack or fear excludes love: "The mind that accepts attack cannot love . . . [and] cannot perceive itself as loving." (T-114) If we actually heard the call of love we could not help but respond and in so doing "the whole world [we] thought [we] made would vanish." (T-226) Through prayer and calling on the Holy Spirit we can let go of fearful thoughts and concentrate on love or God. The Course promises that love " . . . will enter immediately into any mind that truly wants it." (T-55)

Love and joy are equated in the Course and are described as the "only possible whole state." (T-66) Cayce defined divine love by saying "That the Father and the Son, and the Holy Spirit may direct thee, does direct thee, *will* direct thee in every thought, in every act!" (262-104)

Cayce further said, "love divine is that manifested by those in their activities who are guided by love divine. Those bring happiness and the
experiences of joy . . . "(262–111) The two teachings would, therefore,
seem to agree on the definition of love.

Reminding us that we teach ourselves first, ACIM says, "Teach only
love, for that is what you are" (T-87), and "Only by teaching love can
you learn it." (T-92) Cayce's teachings were similar: " . . . As ye give to
others . . . to know more of the Universal Forces, so may ye have the
more, for God is love." (4021–1) So, we are instructed to teach or give out
love in order to increase our awareness of—and identification with—it.
Further, we are told in the Course that our love must be all–encompassing, excluding no one and no thing. Whatever we exclude remains a
projection of guilt and signifies an area that we have not completely
forgiven. " . . . for love cannot enter where there is one spot of fear to
mar its welcome." (T-227) Cayce would seem to agree in reading 3573–1
where he stated:

> Let love be without dissimulation and not so much centralized
> in individuals or personalities, nor in self. Love is universal, as
> God.

If we are to love as God loves we must withhold love from no thing,
no person, no circumstance. Withholding is evidence of the presence of
fear and represents the choice of the ego or the small self to refuse the
all-encompassing experience of God.

Judgment and Forgiveness

*I*n a comparison of the Course and the Cayce teachings it would be unthinkable to exclude the subject of reincarnation and karma, though ACIM does not advocate the former and never uses the word "karma." Cayce incorporated both concepts in the health readings and past life readings.

Cayce taught that life is continuous. We had our birth before time, and we will continue long after the usefulness of the concept of time is gone. Our individual "lifetimes" are associated with particular physical bodies, which represent the densest part of each entity. We choose (or have chosen for us, depending on our development) the family, place, time, and circumstance into which we would incarnate, depending on the experiences needed or debts to be paid (karma), in order to further our growth in consciousness.

> **Each entity must answer for its *own* choosing, as well as for those it has persuaded or prompted in certain directions . . .**
> **For, as one does to others is the measure of greatness or goodness towards the Creative Forces . . .**   **1101-31**

It is every soul's purpose to discover its relationship to God and to manifest the glorification of Creative Forces in the earth. (2487-1) According to the Cayce readings, Jesus, having accomplished this, reached Christ consciousness, and is the pattern for every man in the earth.

For all have the pattern, whether they call on that name or not; but there is no other . . . whereby men may be saved from themselves.   **3528-1**

Jesus, having been Adam, has reincarnated throughout the ages, and there is nothing he has not experienced. (954-5) Therefore, Jesus has already done what we need to accomplish.

ACIM would agree that Jesus was the first to awaken from the dream. However, the Course does not speak of reincarnation and karma as the means of accomplishing this, preferring to keep the student in the present—the only place where he or she can change his or her mind. (M-57) The Course teaches that the mind is the cause, and the entire illusory world is the effect. ACIM would have us learn to let go of all the past because we do not know what any experience or thing was for. True healing can come from releasing and forgiving the past.

On the other hand, we find many passages in the Course that can be interpreted as talking about karma. When we entertained the insane belief that we could usurp the power of God, seeing ourselves as "special" or apart from God, we became guilt-ridden. ACIM states that "(with) the specialness he (humankind) chose to hurt himself did God appoint to be the means for his salvation . . . " (T-493) This would appear to be the use of karma as a teaching device for man. Guilt runs the world we see, and guilt creates karma. Since we identify with the ego, we perceive ourselves as guilty. The main purpose of the Course, therefore, is to teach us how to forgive ourselves for doing something that was impossible to do in the first place—separate ourselves from God.

We do not, as a rule, consciously think about having separated ourselves from God. Instead, we project the guilt outward, upsetting ourselves at apparent wrongs committed by others or ourselves. How often do we find ourselves criticizing another for doing just what we have done or *want* to do? We attach judgments to these "wrongs" we have projected on others. Our judgments are always errors because they are based on illusion. God does not share in these judgments because He is incapable of experiencing illusions of any kind. (T-325) The Course reminds us that any role we give to our brother, we give ourselves. We will go through the same experience because the judgment we laid upon our brother is actually laid upon ourselves. (T-492)

ACIM teaches us that we can go only so far in our efforts to release karma, saying, "You cannot cancel out your errors alone." (T-74) I will elaborate more later about invoking the help of the Holy Spirit in this. We can take inspiration from the Course's promise that "The holiest of all the spots on earth is where an ancient hatred becomes a present love." (T-522) This passage can certainly be interpreted as the release from karma.

The Course teaches that forgiveness is our function in the earth. I had already been through the text of the Course once when this statement finally penetrated my conscious mind. As I re-read the words I realized I was doing nothing in my life to consciously concentrate on forgiveness. Shortly after that I started a forgiveness group at the Houston Center for Attitudinal Healing its purpose being to awaken the need for forgiveness in our everyday lives—and my purpose being to teach what I needed to learn. I have since discovered forgiveness to be a lifelong twofold process. It is necessary to forgive others and myself for the past. At the same time it is necessary to learn to live in a state of acceptance to avoid future need for forgiveness. We can increase our consciousness at both of these levels in the present.

Recall that, according to ACIM, humankind is in the earth because of our belief in the illusion of separation from God and our fellow man. This is at the heart of an underlying guilt, which we all carry, based on our position that we have usurped the power of God. We then think we produced what God's creation lacked, and we believe that we must be punished for having done so. The initial cause of guilt, however, has long been suppressed through denial. We continue to deal with the guilt covertly by projecting it onto the outside world, which we, in our ego mind, made up for this purpose. To do this we invented the idea of sin. Using the sin model we can establish a context of right and wrong so we can see ourselves as right or sin*less* while condemning our brother as wrong or sin*ful*. Robert Perry, in his *Introduction to a Course in Miracles*, defines sin as the "violating of someone or something else for our own benefit."[1] The strategy of the ego in inventing sin, while appearing to condemn others and, thereby, make one feel special and superior, was actually the perpetuation of itself through guilt and self-loathing.

Projection fills our field of vision with guilt, blaming others, the world, God, anything but ourselves, for the sins we secretly believe to be our own.[2]

While we are in ego thinking, or wrong-mindedness, we find sins in others in order to make ourselves feel righteous, but these so-called sins are projections of our own guilt onto our fellow man. This does not make sense of course, but the ego, remember, is insane.

The ego's insane laws were made to guarantee that we would make mistakes, giving them power over us as we accept the results as our due. (T-403) To begin to put a stop to this insane cycle, we have to stop judging and condemning others. The Course reminds us that, indeed, we cannot judge others. We do not have enough evidence, nor do we see the larger picture, so we have no idea of the truth in any situation.

In addition, we can recall the earlier discussion of the mind keeping what it gives out or teaches. The Course's teaching "Never forget you give but to yourself" (W-345) is never more obvious than in the area of judgment and condemnation.

Cayce would concur completely. He said, " . . . with what measure ye mete, with what judgment ye act, so comes it back to thee." (2560-1) He told another seeker "that thou condemnest in another (yea, every man–every woman), that thou becomest in thine self!" (1089-3) In another case, Cayce said, " . . . keep self from condemning any. For, he that would be forgiven must forgive. He that would not be condemned must condemn no one." Further, in the same reading Cayce said:

Condemn not in word, in the thought or activity, that ye be not condemned. See in every expression of activity the attempt of that soul to express and manifest that soul's concept of divine reality.   **262-60**

If we are not spending our time and thoughts in condemnation of others, we are not projecting our own guilt. If we are not projecting guilt, we are accepting what IS and living in the present, open to true vision. When we are in the consciousness of acceptance, we are at peace with our world and ourselves.

Forgiveness gently looks upon all things unknown in Heaven, sees them disappear, and leaves the world a clean and unmarked slate on which the word of God can new replace the senseless symbols written there before. (W–355)

There is no need for forgiveness in that state of mind. ACIM states, "Vision or judgment is your choice, but never both of these." (T–405)

On the other hand, we are carrying with us a heavy burden of guilt and lack of forgiveness from the past, which needs to be addressed. Guilt and lack of forgiveness are our connection with the past, and when not dealt with, they are the creators of the future. In other words, this is the way karma is built.

Recently, it was necessary for me to undergo surgery on my right foot to remove a nerve tumor. A friend offered to take me to the hospital for the outpatient surgery and to take care of me for the few days following the procedure. I noticed that he had a lot of fear about my postsurgical condition, imagining that I would be very ill and require much attention. As it turned out, I did not experience much pain, and it was not necessary that he "nurse" me, as he had expected. However, he insisted on sleeping on the floor *at the foot of my bed*. This went on for three nights, until he was sure I did not require his vigilance.

A month later I was participating in a group hypnosis that was designed to take the audience back to a lifetime in Egypt. Suddenly, I found myself looking down at my feet. I saw two very hairy legs and feet in sandals. I was also aware that I carried a spear and that I was a guard of some kind. Then, I became aware of a pair of very hairy, black legs and feet across from mine, which belonged to another guard. Somehow, I knew these legs belonged to my friend in a lifetime we shared together as slave temple guards in Egypt. Then we began playfully "horsing around," and my friend accidentally wounded my right foot with his spear. This wound resulted in infection, which, eventually, ended that life. My friend, who was my fellow temple guard, never forgave himself for his part in my early death. His insistence in taking care of me in the present after my foot surgery—in a manner that could be said to be that of a slave—would seem to indicate that he felt he must balance that karma.

As mentioned above, *A Course in Miracles* does not address karma, as such, but makes reference to perpetuating the past through lack of forgiveness. The Course states, "Nothing you made has any power over you unless you still would be apart from your Creator." (T-441) The desire for the separation from your Creator is the choice to remain with guilt and the unwillingness to forgive.

Cayce stated that forgiveness is the key to release from the past, or karma:

> **As ye do unto the least of thy brethren, so ye do unto thy Maker. These as laws, as truths, are unfailing. And because He may oft appear slow in meting out the results of such activity does not alter or change the law,** *save as may be understood in the law of forgiveness* **[author's italics].**   **2449-1**

Why do we resist forgiveness? In my counseling with people in this area, there appear to be two common underlying blocks to our willingness to forgive. A popular belief around forgiveness is that doing so is a statement that what the other person did was and is acceptable. Forgiveness is not, however, giving license to another person to continue destructive behavior. Forgiveness allows us to free our hearts to love once again. It does not necessarily change the other person's behavior. The conclusions drawn by the other party involved are between him or her and God. If we recognize that our guilt may have drawn us to a lesson or a mirror of our own past actions or thoughts, then we can choose to get what we need from the situation and quickly return to peace and love.

Another reason we give for resisting forgiveness is that we sometimes believe that to do so would keep another person in our lives or, conversely, allow them to leave. These arguments are merely two sides of the same coin. We tell ourselves that refusing to forgive another will somehow control that person. For example, Jean, a woman who has been repeatedly beaten by her violent husband, feared that forgiving him meant that she would have to allow him back into her life. Another example is the couple, Sarah and Jonah, who refused to forgive their daughter, Lisa, for marrying outside their faith, stating that they would not accept her back into their lives (and inheritance) unless she gave up the marriage and admitted that they were right in their stance. The price they paid for their unwillingness to forgive was life without their daughter and grandchildren to enjoy. The daughter, meanwhile, continues to live her chosen life in relative peace. The parents are the ones who suffer. The Course asks the question, "Would you rather be right or happy?" Somehow, we have the idea that being right makes us happy. However, many times being right makes us separate, and feeling separate is not a happy state of mind.

On the other hand, I became aware, during a recent forgiveness meditation, that I was hesitant to forgive my own daughter, fearing that she would then be free to leave my life. A line in the Course points out, " . . . the ego believes that to forgive another is to lose him." (T-296) What we are trying to do in our lack of forgiveness is to control another person.

Forgiveness is not about the other person(s). It is about our own happiness and peace of mind. The cost of failing to forgive is always the loss of peace of mind on the part of those who refuse to forgive.

If we desire to fulfill our function in the earth, which is, according to ACIM, to forgive, it might be well to remember that whatever we experience is drawn to us for a reason. The Course teaches:

> **I am responsible for what I see.**
> **I choose the feelings I experience, and I decide upon the goal**
> **I would achieve.**
> **And everything that seems to happen to me**
> **I ask for, and receive as I have asked.**
> **(T-418)**

The Course also reminds us that it is impossible for us to be victims.

Our true being, or higher self, as Cayce would term it, is Spirit and, as such, cannot be attacked. Those circumstances that seem to require our forgiveness are illusory in that they concern our *bodies* or emotions, which are not "real." More is said about this in the chapter on healing and the body.

According to ACIM, the process of forgiveness requires that we first forgive our brother, and then forgive ourselves. By doing so we realize that forgiving others, on whom we have projected our guilt, IS forgiving ourselves. Then we call on the Holy Spirit for help in reaching our goal of peace. Asking the Holy Spirit to reinterpret is a way of forgiving. We must be willing to completely release the situation and have the relationship healed. The latter is the Holy Spirit's job.

Cayce echoed this idea when he said, "Yes, forgiveness and karma may at times appear to be extremes; and yet know that *only* in Him—the Christ—do extremes meet." (2449-1) When true forgiveness has taken place we no longer remember the incident and regard our brother with acceptance and unconditional love.

The rewards of forgiveness are happiness and peace of mind as well as release from karma. This may seem remote in our present state of mind. Remember however, that we have been mesmerized by the ego for eons and are just now awakening to a better way. It is important to be patient with yourself and recommit to acceptance and forgiveness every time you find yourself in a judgmental frame of mind. It is self-defeating to produce guilt in yourself for failing to live up to your new understanding. The Course offers a helpful prayer to use in these times:

> I must have decided wrongly, because I am not at peace.
> I made the decision myself, but I can also decide otherwise.
> I want to decide otherwise, because I want to be at peace.
> I do not feel guilty, because the Holy Spirit will undo all the consequences of my wrong decision if I will let Him.
> I choose to let Him, by allowing Him to decide for God for me.
> (T-83)

Relationships: Our Arena of Learning

$\mathcal{M}$ost of my life I have looked outside myself for answers, for fulfillment, for love. I remember thinking that when I graduated from high school and entered college my life would begin. Then I thought, "When I marry my life will surely begin." And then I thought when I started my career and/or my family that my life would begin in earnest. After my divorce I looked for "it" in each relationship with men. If this one was not the right one, surely the next one would be, and my REAL life would begin. Needless to say, with my constant search outside myself for meaning in life and a sense of completion, I was never satisfied. As my search turned inward, however, through the insights found in the Cayce material, I discovered that what I was looking for had to be found within, through contact with spirit. This did not automatically ensure that I would cease looking outward for answers and fulfillment. Habits of several lifetimes are hard to break! I did become vigilant of my thoughts and, utilizing daily meditation and prayer began training myself to seek God's light and guidance.

Still, when I discovered *A Course in Miracles* I found I had far to go in learning to turn every decision over to the Holy Spirit or God. This was especially noticeable in relationships, where I continued to change out the people if the relationships did not seem to fulfill my needs. My own marriage was typical. I felt as if my second husband wanted a tomato and I was a kumquat. When I traded in my "kumquatness," in an effort to be the tomato he wanted, I felt resentful and inadequate. On the other hand, I had given up on him being the true partner I sought, so I fulfilled my perceived needs through other friendships, never quite satisfied and somehow blaming my husband. Always in the back of my mind was the belief that if I just found the "right" partner everything would be changed. This scenario is not unusual in this modern age. Until I encountered the Course, however, I did not realize that what was lacking was a sense of completion, which could only be found in my returning to the Source. My feeling of missing something came from the separation so often mentioned in ACIM, symbolized by the fall of man in the Bible and in the Cayce material.

The Course teaches that "whatever reminds you of your past grievances attracts you, and seems to go by the name of love . . . " (T-330) This explains why we sometimes find ourselves in uncomfortable relationships. Both Edgar Cayce's readings and *A Course in Miracles* teach that relationships provide the most fertile area for better understanding ourselves. Cayce told us that the way we treat our brother reflects our relationship with our Maker, and he often quoted the biblical commandment that we love one another. Therefore, any discussion of relationships has to include our understanding of love and its expression in our lives.

The Course talks about love as being part of the process of atonement and, in that context, something that cannot be taught. As mentioned earlier, it also refers to love as an emotion, and according to ACIM there are only two emotions: love and fear.

ACIM has much to say about two kinds of relationships: "special relationships" and "holy relationships." A special relationship is any relationship with another person, place, or thing that we believe will give us something we lack. Keeping in mind that, from the perspective of the Course, God created his Son perfect and lacking nothing, our belief that we need anything or anyone is a declaration that we believe we are separate from God. " . . . to experience yourself as alone is to deny the Oneness of the Father and His Son, and thus attack reality." (T-290) Looking at it this way, all that we see or seek represents our belief in separation. When we seek out a relationship with another person, the ego part of our minds is defining our own needs and looking outside ourselves, outside God's creation, and attempting to satisfy the perceived needs on our own terms. This solution involves limitation, as we confine our loving to a part of the Sonship. It is an attempt to use separation to save ourselves. Therefore, all relationships formed on this basis represent our belief in lack and separation from God. The Holy Spirit uses the special relationships we have devised as learning experiences to lead us to truth. With the help of the Holy Spirit every relationship can become a lesson in love. (T-291) When we become aware that we are participating in a special relationship we can offer it to the Holy Spirit for purification and for His use. He will bring the relationship into the present, releasing it from the past where the ego used it to judge our brothers.

The holy relationship, on the other hand, is one that is not based on lack. Its purpose is forgiveness and healing through the joining of minds. With each holy relationship comes communication instead of separation (T-437) and the power to heal all pain, no matter what form. (T-438) We choose for our relationships to be holy whenever we choose joining rather than separation, when we seek the good of all rather than the fulfillment of a perceived need of our own, created by the ego.

The popular term for special relationships in today's psychological vocabulary is that of the "co-dependant" relationship. This is a relationship in which both parties are intertwined in need and guilt, both supporting the other's continued contract to stay dependent, and therefore, controlled or possessed by the other. Edgar Cayce seems to be addressing the special relationship when he admonishes,

> **Let love be without dissimulation—that is without possession
> . . . but, as . . . He gave, 'Love one another, even as I have loved
> you'; willing to give the life, the self for the [higher] purpose . . .**
>
> **413-11**

Cayce seemed to be speaking of a holy relationship when he said that in true, pure love there is less personal desire and more patience.

When love is present in a relationship it does not diminish when shared with others. He said, " . . . when an individual has a friend that is lovely to him, to make other friendships does not lesson the love for the other." (696-3) On the other hand, the presence of distress, anxiety, pain, jealousy, doubt, or fear signifies what the Course would call a special relationship, and what Cayce called body–consciousness, being of the small self or ego. (696-3) Cayce pointed out that relationships that serve selfish desires or self-exaltation do not promote a closer relationship with Creative Forces or God. (1096-1)

No mention of the marital relationship per se is made in the Course. One could conclude, however, that the majority of marriages reflect the special relationship model. This does not mean that ACIM is against marriage, as one troubled woman told me. Any special relationship has the potential of becoming a holy relationship. All that is required is that the participants change their minds and commit the relationship to the purposes of the Holy Spirit. We cannot conclude that doing so, however, will make a relationship that is problem–free. There would be no growth or awakening without challenges. What will happen in a holy relationship is that the partners will mirror for one another. In other words, when one is caught up in the world of form, failing to see beyond a particular problem, the partner can be there to demonstrate joining, to look beyond the form to the level where their minds can be joined. Problems in the world can be traced back to the belief in and fear of separation. When we are caught up in a problem we do not know the truth as to why we are upset. We believe it is the form, or what seems to be going on "out there" when it is actually our belief in the separation that has us upset.

Cayce suggested that we could use the marital or family relationship to practice for a heavenly existence. In other words, in our most intimate relationships we can give unconditional love and develop the kind of relationships we think would be appropriate in heaven. "Let the light of love in, then, to the heart that is seeking the Love of the Christ." (1215-4) In another reading Cayce pointed out that "love is giving, and the spirit of same is NEVER demanding." (1703-3) In a line similar to the Course's "All that I give is given to myself," Cayce said "only that ye give away do ye possess." (1786.2) This is especially appropriate when said about love.

The Course defines love as joining while fear is separating. Another way to put it is that if we are not loving, we are calling for love. It makes it easier to deal with those we meet if we keep this in mind. In my classroom I try to remind myself of this when a child misbehaves. If I can get in touch with the idea that the child is calling for love rather than attacking me or another child, I remember to call on the Holy Spirit to help me see the situation or child differently. This gets my ego out of the way long enough for love and peace energy to come through. Then, I find myself extending love rather than pulling it in closely as if that could provide protection. Put in more metaphysical terms, I find when I extend my energy field, known as the aura, it includes the frightened child, who is then comforted. Extending the energy field of love surrounding me also provides a buffer zone that reminds me to identify with love rather than defensiveness. I experience this by giving love to myself while offering it to others. What I give to others is what I keep.

Again, the Course does not concentrate on behavior or form. Its teachings on relationships all have to do with changing the mind concerning the purpose of the relationship. Though Cayce taught similarly, always reminding us to set the ideal and let it influence our thoughts and actions, he also gave individual advice for improving relationships. He often referred to past life experiences while explaining present circumstances, reminding us that we are always meeting ourselves. When we encounter difficulties in relationships we can always ask ourselves what the relationship partner is mirroring for us—what have we projected onto another person in order to see it in ourselves?

I recall a student, Frieda, who I found to be very annoying because she continuously interrupted my lessons. In addition she repeatedly interfered with the other children and seemed unable to mind her own business. After I realized that she was mirroring one of my perceived faults, that of failing to mind my own business, I no longer found her irritating. Frieda continued her antisocial behavior but it had lost its power to upset me. Mentally, I thanked her for being willing to be my mirror.

At one time, during a brief attempt to work in the business world, I had a hectic and difficult job that required more of me than I could provide. I had an unofficial supervisor who would not share information freely. One day I overheard him discussing some work that would be required of the people I supervised. When I asked him for details, he shouted, "Go to your desk, sit down and be quiet!" Instead of reacting with anger, as I formerly would have, I had a sudden realization that he was mirroring the way I had in the past been known to treat unruly students. With that realization I knew I had received what I had come for in that job situation. Within two weeks I was relieved to leave the job.

This kind of mirroring, which leads to self-discovery, is available to the seeker who is ready to find a better way to live and be. Study of the Cayce philosophy opened the door for me to know myself better.

The Course, which teaches that there is no order of difficulty in miracles, simplifies the task of self-knowing by advocating that there is only one source of difficulty, that of believing in the separation from God and the resultant guilt. Accordingly, the insight and solution remain the same. We are to recognize that the discomfort we experience comes from the belief in the separation and remember to ask the Holy Spirit to help us see the situation in a different way. Forgiveness of self and others is always involved in this process. We can utilize all sorts of relationships to remind us of our separation beliefs and practice turning over our relationships or our "problems" to the Holy Spirit.

It is not likely we will ever be totally free of special relationships while in the third dimensional life on earth. However, we can become more aware and commit ourselves to continuously dedicating our relationships to God's purposes. Cayce defined divine love as " . . . that the Father and the Son and the Holy Spirit may direct thee . . . in every thought, in every act." (262-104)

While the Course would have us release any belief or attachment that holds us to the illusory world, it does seem to agree with the Cayce material in that relationships can be utilized as a means of joining with God's purposes for His Sonship.

Drawing Closer to God
Through Prayer and Meditation

Cayce placed great importance on the regular practices of prayer and meditation, describing them as a method of connecting with the infinite through the higher self within. He recommended meditation as beneficial for most everyone, and gave detailed instructions on how to meditate and use affirmations for mind focus. Cayce defined prayer as talking to God and meditation as listening to God.

The Course declares that prayer can be the "medium of miracles" when it is a means of communication of the created with the Creator. (T–1) However, most of what people call prayer is petitionary and, therefore, a part of the world of perception and illusion. Most prayers ask God for something we believe we lack. The only true prayer, according to ACIM, is for forgiveness, because when we have forgiveness we have everything. (T–40)

The Course does not explicitly discuss meditation. However, the lessons from the ACIM Workbook can be seen as training the mind for meditation. Each lesson begins with an affirmation appropriate for mind focus, and the more advanced lessons even mention quieting the mind, i.e. Lesson 125: "In quiet I receive God's Word today." (W–220) In lesson 189 we are told,

> Be still, and lay aside all thoughts of what you are and what God
> is . . . Forget this world, forget this Course, and come with
> wholly empty hands unto your God. (W-350)

This is a beautiful and effective directive for meditation. Therefore, it can be argued that ACIM does teach the value and practice of meditation, whether or not it utilizes the term.

In the Search For God study groups, which meet all over the world, Cayce students practice prayer and meditation both within the group and as a personal daily endeavor. Prayer is defined in the Search for God material as "the concerted effort of our physical consciousnesses to become attuned to the Consciousness of the Creator."[1] This sounds very much like the definition found in the Course, mentioned previously. In my own experience, in preparing to meditate, I find prayers of gratitude to be most helpful. I spend a few minutes thanking God for not only the good in my life but also the opportunities for growth that are before me. This quickly puts me into a receptive frame of mind for my meditation. Some people find ritual prayers to be helpful, and recite them as mantras. The "Lord's Prayer" can be a ritual prayer, or, according to Cayce, it can be used thoughtfully as a means of opening the spiritual centers, which connect the physical body to its spiritual counterpart. I have revised the original prayer to reflect the teachings of the Course as follows:

Our Father who art everywhere
Hallowed by thy name.
Thy kingdom is here.
Thy will is being done
in earth as it is in heaven.
Thou art giving us this day
our daily bread
and forgiving us
even as we have forgiven others.
Thou art leading us out of the dream
and delivering us from the ego.

**For thine is the kingdom and the
power and the glory forever.**

When using the prayer before meditation, do not follow it with "amen" as that has the effect of closing the spiritual centers.

If I am particularly agitated during my time of prayer and meditation, I use prayers as a way of talking it out with God until I reach a more peaceful state of mind. If there is ANY area in my life requiring forgiveness I direct prayers to healing that situation until I feel peaceful. The Bible admonishes us not to approach the altar if we have anything against our brother. We are advised to first make peace with our brother (Matthew 5:23). If we interpret the "altar" as the holy place within, to which we go when we meditate, it is clear that we are being called upon to forgive. Cayce certainly believed this, warning that to enter meditation without preparation could result in creating other than optimum results. Cayce taught, "When meditation is properly entered into, we are made stronger mentally and physically."[2] Prayer was certainly a major part of the preparation for meditation. It may also be utilized after meditation as a means of directing the energies raised to help others.

In our Search for God study groups we keep a list of people who have asked for our help. After meditation we mention these people by name, directing the light energy to them for their good. It is important that the energy be disseminated, as failure to do so can result in headaches or other forms of imbalance. We do not, however, direct the energy to people who have NOT asked for help because to do so would interfere with their free will. I had a personal experience with this in my first study group.

Our group had added the name of an ill child to our list of people to whom we sent energy for healing. During the following week , four out of the group of ten members had dreams in which the boy came to us saying in various ways that if we continued to pray for his healing he would have to leave the earth. His illness had a purpose in healing his relationship with his father. Needless to say, we were very hesitant to direct the energy without request after that.

Cayce said that there are as many forms of meditation as there are people in the earth. Therefore, any effort to meditate is counted as righ-teousness. Some people get discouraged if their meditation doesn't match the experience of someone else. People sometimes let expecta-tions get in the way, perhaps asking, "Shouldn't I be seeing white light by now?" If we have a mindset as to what the meditation experience should be we defeat our purpose. We have not really given ourselves over to the experience of God on His terms. The important thing is to make the effort daily and wait on God for the "increase," or results.

The effort to meditate begins with setting the ideal (more will be said of this subsequently). It is important to establish the best time of day for meditation and keep the appointment. Cayce instructed that we center ourselves, pray to reach the right frame of mind, attune to the Whole by entering the "holy of holies," or that place of knowing within, and then sit in silence for a period of time. Cayce described sitting in the silence as a period of active listening, as if every cell of the body is focused on hearing God. This process energizes the spiritual centers of the physical and spiritual bodies, allowing energy to be raised up the kundalini path-way, in the area of the spine. After the energy is raised up it is then directed outward in service to others. The energy can continue to be directed outward as long as the meditator feels the flow. As the energy subsides, the meditator can return to prayers of thanksgiving. The medi-tation is ended with a conscious closing of the spiritual centers so that they return to normal operation.

The concept of "setting the ideal," as mentioned previously, was an important process recommended by Cayce for all. The ideal, as used in the Cayce material, is the pattern "by which we endeavor to shape our lives."[3] It is a merging of our physical and mental ideals with that of the soul. Our true ideal, then, is "the highest spiritual attainment to be reached on this material plane."[4] Cayce taught that this would be found in the Christ who is the Way. (The Course would agree in that we must do as He did who recognized the reality of the Eternal Oneness, which has never been broken.) How we word our ideal is up to us, but it should be of a spiritual nature. Once we have set our ideal we use it as a guide and yardstick to all that we do, especially meditation. If we have set our ideal too low we can misdirect the spiritual energy, creating more problems for others or ourselves. Choosing the ideal should not be taken lightly. It is a decision that should be made with much prayer and guidance from within.

Utilizing Dream Guidance

One of the results of setting an ideal is that we begin to get help from other levels of consciousness. Edgar Cayce placed much importance on utilizing dream guidance as a way of better knowing ourselves. Increased, purposeful prayer and meditation practice will also bring about increased awareness of dream activity. As we make the decision to take advantage of that resource, our dreams take on new importance. Dreams can offer us guidance in our daily lives for everything from diet to relationships. Through the study of our dreams we may gain insight into everyday challenges at work or in the home as well as receive guidance in our spiritual journey. Cayce taught that every person, place, or thing in our dreams is symbolic of the self. He viewed the dream as a message from the unconscious, so the language had to be symbolic. He boldly stated that every important event in our lives is previewed in our dreams. Members of Search for God study groups keep dream journals and often spend time during their weekly meetings sharing dreams for help in gaining insights. Group input is important since we as individuals often do not wish to face the information provided by the dream. The dreamer, however, is the final authority on the message of the dream, and usually recognizes when it has been discovered.

Carrying the concept a bit further, I find it useful to analyze my so-called waking life in terms of dream symbolism when trying to discover the lesson in my life experiences. Many times this gives additional insight. For example, a few years ago I was experiencing a long period of unemployment. I was concentrating my efforts on getting a teaching job in a different city and had gotten no results. Over a period of two weeks I had the uncomfortable experience of my car being bumped from behind by other vehicles THREE TIMES! There was no real damage involved so I was able to focus on the idea that these experiences could carry a message. I decided to analyze the experience as if it were a dream. The message then seemed to be to "get moving"—which made sense with the school year beginning in less than a month. Following this advice I began making efforts to find a teaching job locally and was successful within two weeks.

A Course in Miracles does not assign a value to dreams at all. It states, "Dreams are chaotic because they are governed by your conflicting wishes, and therefore they have no concern with what is true." (T-350) Recall, additionally, that the Course regards all of our existence here as a dream experience which has already ended, though we are unaware that it HAS ended. There would be nothing to gain, from the perspective of Course teachings, from assigning meaning or value to dream symbols or anything else that makes the illusion seem real. Obviously, there is no correlation between the two teachings on the value of dreams.

And in the End

The views of the Cayce material and that of the Course are similar concerning death. Both proclaim that there is no death of that which is real—the soul or Spirit. What dies is the physical body, which is not the part of us that is eternal.

Cayce said, " . . . it isn't all of life to live in one experience. For, life is continued; life itself is a consciousness . . . "(2399-1) Death in the material realm is birth into the spiritual or non-material realm. (369-3) Cayce made some interesting references to the experiences of life immediately after death of the body as dependent on our consciousness. According to Cayce, some souls spend a considerable amount of time between lives in the equivalent of sleeping. Others wander the earth for years, not knowing they are dead. Many pass into what is known as the astral plane, where they experience a reality created from their emotions and thoughts. Cayce observed at one point, in viewing these souls on the astral plane, that it was hard to tell the difference between what they had actually done in life and what they had just thought.

We are encouraged by Cayce to pray for the departed so that they recognize their status, and so that those who love them can minister unto them. On the other hand, Cayce warned against praying in such a way as to inhibit their departure from the physical plane.

When questioned about heaven Cayce's response was:

> For as the Teacher of teachers gave, the Kingdom of heaven is within Thee! and as ye make within thine own consciousness, through thy dwelling upon the thoughts of Him who is the Way, who is the Truth, who is the Light . . .   1759-1

In other words, we must learn to be in touch with the kingdom of heaven within in order to be aware of that consciousness when we pass from the material world. We do not change consciousness just because we no longer inhabit a physical body.

When asked about suicide Cayce's response was to say that we do not have the right to end our life as long as anyone still needs us:

> [Suicide is wrong] So long as there are those that depend upon the body! . . . No man liveth to himself, no man dieth to himself. No man hath been so low that some soul hath not depended upon, relied upon same for strength.   1175-1

We are reminded that our choices affect others and, due to the ripple effect, the consciousness of all.

Since ACIM teaches that all temporal things, including the body, are illusions, one might presume that suicide would not be wrong. However, according to the Course, even when we have awakened from the dream we will not leave our earthly life until God wills it. Conversely, the Course also teaches, "No one can die unless he chooses death." (T-388)

We are reminded that ACIM says that the Holy Spirit regards the body as a neutral teaching device and uses it for communication. The ego uses the body as proof of separation, creating a fence. (W-415) The body serves whichever purpose we choose. While we are in the dream, we fear communication and welcome death as the "silencer of the Voice that speaks for God." (T-389) Of course, death does not end the conflict. Only when we are willing to return to our awareness of the oneness does the conflict end. We are promised that when we give up the "exaltation" of the body in favor of the spirit we will discover that we love spirit beyond our ability to love the body. "Love Itself has called". (T-392) " . . . and your heart will be so filled with joy that it will leap into Heaven." (T-185)

Cayce taught that we enter Heaven on the arm of one we have helped. Similarly, the Course says that the "Arc of Peace is entered two by two." (T-404) Put more strongly, "Forsake not now your brother . . . Either you give each other life or death; either you are each other's savior or his judge, offering him sanctuary or condemnation." (T-440) The two teachings then, seem to agree that our brother's return to the source is equally important to our own. Cayce pointed out that we eventually reach a point in our development where reincarnation is no longer necessary. However, by then, most of us return to help our brothers and sisters, realizing that the journey is not complete until all have accomplished it. When we return we will "know ourselves to be ourselves, yet one with God." (3003-1)

In the view of ACIM the return of the Son to His Father was complete at the moment that one Son awakened because there IS only one Son. Jesus already achieved this awakening. For this reason, He can be said to be the "savior" of us all. However, the remainder of us who still believe in the dream and separation are caught up in the illusion. Jesus, therefore, can be said to maintain one foot in the illusion and one foot in heaven, offering Himself as a means of escape for those who begin to awaken. One way of doing this was to provide *A Course in Miracles*. Jesus, as author of the Course, assures us that He takes the journey with us, while still holding in His mind the way out. His resurrection is renewed every time one of us completes the journey and forgets the dream. (W-322) The Holy Spirit is our mediator between illusion and truth. (W-427) The Holy Spirit's goal is to end our dreams by carrying them to truth. "Together we will disappear into the Presence beyond the veil, not to be lost but found; not to be seen but known." (T-395)

The End Times

The Cayce readings referred to the turn of the twenty-first century as the new millennium when Jesus was expected to return. Cayce predicted drastic earth changes, which would possibly annihilate more than half the population on the planet. This could be followed by the "thousand years of peace" predicted in the Book of Revelations. Many regard this event as the "end of the world as we know it." The earth changes are viewed not as some sort of punishment for mankind, but as adjustments made on the planet in order to maintain balance. That some of the imbalance is due to man's selfish nature and misuse of earth's resources is a concept that appears in the Cayce readings.

The expectancy of the Prince of Peace coming again into the earth, as predicted in the Bible, is seen as a real, physical possibility in the Cayce readings. This, however, does not preclude the concept of the "second coming" also being an inner event, wherein the individual accepts Christ into his or her heart.

According to the Course, Christ is God's Son, the Self we share, and He has not left his "holy home." Christ is our link with God. (W–421) "The Second Coming of Christ means nothing more than the end of the ego's rule and the healing of the mind." (T–58) God did not create the world as we see it because He creates only that which is eternal. The loving thoughts of the Son of God are this world's only reality. Any ideas we have had that are unloving and separating are the world of illusion. "The real world is all that the Holy Spirit has saved for you out of what you have made, and to perceive only this is salvation." (T–195)

The Course points out that the world we see is perceived through the eyes of fear and, being an illusion, will end in an illusion of mercy. Forgiveness will end guilt, which made the world. When no thoughts of sin remain, the illusion of the world will be gone. In a most memorable line we are told, "It will merely cease to seem to be." (M–35) This reminds us that the world and life we cling to is but an illusion. "The end of the world is not its destruction, but its translation into Heaven. The reinterpretation of the world is the transfer of all perception to knowledge." (T–196)

Conclusion

Some have said that *A Course in Miracles* and the Cayce teachings can not be used together, though people all over the United States *are* using both resources. I hope this book has made it easier for the student to see where and how the two teachings do and do not support each other.

The scribe of the Course, Helen Schucman, was interested in the subject of reincarnation and had apparently studied the Cayce material because of this. She was warned by Jesus against a continued belief in the concepts of reincarnation and karma because they are linked to the linear view of time, and prevented her from focusing on the present.[1] The student of both teachings can keep this warning in mind as a reminder to continue to live and focus in the present. On the other hand, Kenneth Wapnick notes in his book, *Absence From Felicity*, a message to Helen that was not included in the Course text and which came from Jesus. This message stated (in connection with Cayce), that, "out of respect for his great efforts on My behalf I would not let his life-work lead to anything but truth in the end."[2]

I have not attempted to cover every aspect of the two teachings. Edgar Cayce touched on almost every facet of life on the physical, mental, and spiritual levels, though not always in depth. Both topics and details depended on questions asked at the time the readings were being conducted. Space does not allow consideration of all of these topics. Much material can be gleaned from the Cayce readings regarding mystical experiences, psychic abilities, levels of consciousness, and heavenly beings, such as angels. ACIM ignores all of these subjects except for psychic powers, which it acknowledges in the *Teacher's Manual*. (M-59) This can be disconcerting to the student who has experienced the mystical realm and who might think the Course is discounting such experiences. Those who have had mystical experiences often have no doubts about their validity. Perhaps it could be said that ACIM is aimed at the beginner who is unlikely to have had such experiences. Those who have not had mystical experiences, such as visions, visits by angels, etc., might be quick to judge them to be illusions of the ego. An advocate of the Course teachings could argue that Spirit does not come into the illusion and participate in it. Therefore, this could be considered an area in which Cayce and the Course cannot be reconciled.

The Course is intended to be a teaching for the mind and does not address behavior in the world of matter. Both Cayce and the Bible, to which Cayce often refers as an authority, focus a great deal of attention on our behavior in the world and towards our fellow travelers. Cayce's teachings address the physical, mental, and spiritual levels, encompassing every aspect of humankind's experience in the third dimension. ACIM, on the other hand, continuously reminds us that the material world is unreal and only the result of our beliefs. Cayce taught that we should bring the spiritual into our lives and into the world. The Course says this cannot be done because the world is only a dream.

Taking all this into account, the student can utilize the Cayce teachings as a means of understanding the overall picture, then use this understanding to take responsibility for present circumstances and for creating a better future. The Course's perspective adds a focus on forgiveness as a means of releasing our investment in the dream of materiality. Both teach that we will not be complete until we are reunited with God, recognizing our true status in the creation. Any teaching that encourages us to step back and view ourselves, "watching self go by," as Cayce put it, is helpful in returning us to our true home, in the "journey without distance to a goal that has never changed." (T-139)

Endnotes

Introduction
1. "Liberalism and Conservatism in the Course Community," by Robert Perry. *Miracles Magazine*, #4, p. 31.
2. *Absence from Felicity*, by Kenneth Wapnick, p. 1. Published in 1991, 1999 by Foundation for *A Course in Miracles*, Roscoe, NY.

In the Beginning
1. *A Million Years to the Promised Land*, Robert Krajenke, Prologue, xxi.
2. Ibid, xxii.
3. Ibid, xxiii.

The Nature of Mind
1. *The Edgar Cayce Primer*, by Bruce Puryear, Bantam Books, 1982, p. 59.
2. *A Search for God, Book I*, A.R.E., p. 41.
3. Op Cit, Perry, p. 23.

Judgment and Forgiveness
1. *An Introduction to a Course in Miracles*, by Robert Perry, Miracles Distribution Center, 1989, p. 22.
2. Ibid. p. 24.

Drawing Closer to God Through Meditation and Prayer
1. *A Search for God, Book I*, p. 5.
2. Ibid, p. 6.
3. Ibid, p. 41.
4. Ibid, p. 44.

Conclusion
1. Wapnick, Kenneth, *Absence From Felicity*, p. 295.
2. Ibid, p. 296.

A.R.E. PRESS

The A.R.E. Press publishes books, videos, and audiotapes meant to improve the quality of our readers' lives—personally, professionally, and spiritually. We hope our products support your endeavors to realize your career potential, to enhance your relationships, to improve your health, and to encourage you to make the changes necessary to live a loving, joyful, and fulfilling life.

For more information or to receive a free catalog, call:

1–800–723–1112

Or write:

A.R.E. Press
215 67th Street
Virginia Beach, VA 23451–2061

DISCOVER HOW THE EDGAR CAYCE MATERIAL CAN HELP YOU!

The Association for Research and Enlightenment, Inc. (A.R.E.®), was founded in 1931 by Edgar Cayce. Its international headquarters are in Virginia Beach, Virginia, where thousands of visitors come year-round. Many more are helped and inspired by A.R.E.'s local activities in their own hometowns or by contact via mail (and now the Internet!) with A.R.E. headquarters.

People from all walks of life, all around the world, have discovered meaningful and life-transforming insights in the A.R.E. programs and materials, which focus on such areas as personal spirituality, holistic health, dreams, family life, finding your best vocation, reincarnation, ESP, meditation, and soul growth in small-group settings. Call us today at our toll-free number:

1-800-333-4499

or

Explore our electronic visitors center on the
Internet: **http://www.edgarcayce.org.**

We'll be happy to tell you more about how the work of the A.R.E. can help you!

A.R.E.
215 67th Street
Virginia Beach, VA 23451-2061